The publisher wishes to thank
«Les Olivades», for the cover design,
which is part of the **Bonis** collection.

CARRÉS
GOURMANDS

© ÉDITIONS ÉQUINOXE, 1998
Domaine de Fontgisclar, Draille de Magne
13570 BARBENTANE

ISBN 2-84135-124-6
ISSN 1276-4416

Cuisine and Recipes from Provence

CLAIRE LHERMEY
Illustrations by Lizzie Napoli

TRANSLATION BY JULIE ROSSINI

TYPOGRAPHIE & MISE EN PAGES : YVES PERROUSSEAUX

ÉQUIN●XE

Cuisine and Recipes from Provence

A subtle scent is coming out of the kitchen, and transforms itself into a powerful perfume. It is the result of the glorious union of garlic and olive oil, and today, the guests are the aromatic herbs from the guarrigue, and their cousins the vegetables. The scent is filling out, taking shape, surrounding you, hurling you down in the world of a sunny and rich Cuisine, as reassuring and warm as a childhood memory.

Outside, the cicadas are calling for you. The table is laid under the vine arbour and the rosé, bought at the local cooperative, is cooling down.

On the tablecloth, made of printed calico, a fougasse and a few dishes of olives and tapenade are revealed.

Menu

CHAPTER 6

Summer dishes

CHAPTER 1

Flavours setting the tune

*I*F one had to summarise the Provencal cuisine putting its smells, flavours, and tastes into worlds, the story might begin :
Once upon a time, there was garlic, olive oil, tomato and thyme...

- *Aïoli,* Garlic mayonnaise
- *Anchoïade,* Anchovies, and olive pommade
- *Pistou,* Pesto
- *Tapenade,* Anchovy cream
- *Rouille,*
- *Coulis de tomates,* Tomato sauce
- *Câprade,*
- *Ail en chemise* Garlic puree.

Aïoli
Garlic mayonnaise

*I*F one had to recommend only one Provencal dish, it would have to be aïoli, a divine union of egg, garlic and olive oil, rich in symbolism. This sauce, which has now become a dish in its full right, is delightful at Christmas, as well as during the summer.

N.B. *All the ingredients have to be at room temperature.*

Take half a dozen cloves of garlic, an egg yolk, one to two bowls of olive oil, and salt and pepper.

Pound the garlic with a pestle in a mortar so as to obtain a thin paste, add salt pepper and the egg yolk.

Continuing to stir, pour with the other hand a thin trickle of olive oil, with a few drops of water if needs be, so as to get a firm and fine sauce. The pestle should really be able to stand in the sauce, which is the indubitable sign of success.

The aïoli is served with cooked vegetables, such as potatoes, carrots, green beans and cauliflower and, according to your taste, cod, whelks or snails.

It is possible to get a quick mayonnaise, very inferior to the first, but sometimes useful however, by mixing canned mayonnaise, garlic powder and olive oil.

Tapenade
Anchovies, and olive pommade

*T*HE tapenade can be appreciated at every moment of the day : on toast to eat with an aperitif, with crudités, with hard-boiled eggs, or with goat's cheese. Some people even have it for breakfast.

Take 200 g/7 oz of black olives, with the stones taken out, the same amount of capers, a can of anchovies, and another of tuna, then a tablespoonful of Dijon mustard, a small glass of olive oil, some pepper and a few drops of cognac.

Pound the first ingredients (olives, capers and fish) with a pestle, or, more easily, using a blender.

Thicken with the mustard and enough oil to obtain a pommade. Season with the pepper and cognac. If it's not all eaten in the first sitting, store in the fridge, in air tight containers.

Pistou
Pesto

THIS basil sauce is traditionally served in a «pistou soup» (see page 40), but it is equally delicious when served with pasta or green beans.

Take two or three cloves of garlic, some fresh basil leaves, some grated cheese or Parmesan, olive oil, and one skinned, seeded and chopped tomato if you like.

Pound the garlic in a mortar, adding the chopped basil leaves, the grated cheese, the tomato (if necessary) and enough olive oil – about the quantity of a small glass – to obtain a creamy sauce.

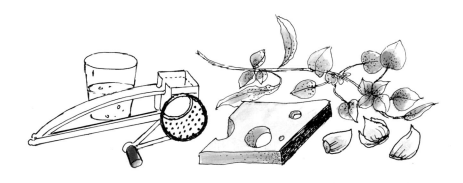

Anchoïade
Anchovy cream

TAKE one small jar of salted anchovies, one or two cloves of garlic, a drop of vinegar, some black pepper, fresh from the mill, and a drop of olive oil.

Remove all the bones from the anchovies. Clean them and leave them in fresh water for a few minutes. Meanwhile, prepare the accompaniment.

For a snack or an appetizer, toast the bread on a wood fire if possible. For a starter, prepare an assortment of fresh vegetables, like bunches of cauliflower, broccoli, celery, heads of chicory, or sticks of carrots, to which boiled eggs might be added.

Sweat the anchovies in a thick saucepan on a slow heat and while stirring, add the pounded garlic, the pepper, the vinegar, and enough oil to give the sauce a smooth and thick consistency.

Serve warm or cold in a bowl, and season if necessary : you may have to add some more salt.

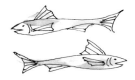

Rouille

*T*HIS sauce is mainly used in the bouillabaisse (see p. 19), but it is also delicious served with a soupe du pêcheur (fish soup), cold or warm fish, or any kind of sea food.

Take two cloves of garlic, two small red chillies, a «handful» of bread without the crust, a cup of milk, two tablespoons of olive oil, and a little fish stock.

Soak the bread in the milk. Pound the garlic in a mortar, with the seeded chillies.

Add the squeezed bread and keep on pounding while gently pouring over it the olive oil, and the stock. The sauce should have the consistency of a mayonnaise.

Coulis de tomates
Tomato sauce

*T*AKE *one or two kg/4,5 lb of tomatoes, two or three onions, and garlic cloves, some olive oil, salt and pepper. You will also need some aromatic herbs, as you think you will like, such as thyme, bay leaves, rosemary, parsley, and basil, as well as two lumps of sugar in case the tomatoes turn out not to be sweet enough.*

Skin the tomatoes, then chop them. Place them in a frying pan with a drop of olive oil, the garlic, the chopped onions, and the sugar if necessary. Leave to simmer for about an hour, stirring frequently, and crush with a fork.

Reduce over a slow heat if the coulis is still too liquid.

The coulis can be served either cold or warm. It can be frozen or preserved in sterilised jars.

Câprade

HIS caper sauce (called « tapeno » in Provence) might be served with fish, or squid as well as courgettes/zucchinis and aubergines/eggplants.

Take one onion, a small glass of olive oil, a small glass of coulis de tomates, a tablespoon of plain flour, a drop of stock (either fish or meat according to which dish the sauce will be served with), a small jars of capers, and a drop of vinegar.

In a small casserole dish, gently sweat the chopped onion and add the flour. Mix with the coulis, and a drop of stock. Let it simmer for a few minutes.

Add capers and vinegar, just before serving.

Ail en chemise
Garlic puree

THE "ail en chemise" is the puree that comes from cooked cloves of garlic. It is as sweet and smooth as raw garlic is hot and spicy and it can be served with roasted meat, or spread on toasted bread. An alternative is to add some chopped anchovies and a drop of vinegar to it.

It can be cooked in different ways :

In embers : The garlic cloves placed in the ashes of an extinguished fire make the best puree of garlic. Once cooked, lightly squeeze each clove to let the puree out.

Stuffing : Cloves cooked in a dish or inside poultry. (See page 80.)

In water : Cloves cooked in salted boiling water for twenty minutes. After the cloves have cooked for ten minutes, add pasta shells to the water. The cloves will give them a nice flavour.

CHAPTER 2

Salads and starters

*I*N Provence, we serve salads as starters, as they enhance our appetite. Some of them are large enough to be served as a light meal : the salade niçoise, the salad camarguaise, the pissaladière, for example, or the caillettes.

- *Salade niçoise,*
- *Salade tiède de pois chiches,* Warm chickpea salad
- *Salade fère ou salade sauvage,* Wild salad
- *Salade camarguaise,*
- *Caviar d'aubergines,* Aubergine/Eggplant "caviar"
- *Caillettes,*
- *Pissaladière,* Onion tart
- *Papeton d'aubergines,*
- *Fougasse aux olives.*

allongés
à l'huile

Hui

Salade niçoise

THOUGH it originally comes from Nice, this has now been around the world, and has been prepared according to many variations.
Here is a classical one.

For two, you will need : 4 tomatoes, half a cucumber, half a pepper, two small artichokes, one hard-boiled egg, one small onion, a few «olives niçoises» (black ones will do if you can't find the niçoises), as well as a few anchovies.
For the seasoning : garlic, lemon juice, salt and fresh pepper.

Wash the vegetables and prepare them by sweating both the tomatoes and the cucumber for an hour with salt.

Cut the tomatoes, the artichokes and the boiled egg into four pieces, and the cucumber, the onion, and the pepper into thin strips.
Rub a salad bowl with a garlic clove.

Add salt, pepper, the lemon juice, and the olive oil, then neatly place the vegetables. Finally, add the boiled eggs, the anchovies, and the olives, placing them nicely on top of the rest. Stir when served.

Salade tiède de pois chiches

Warm chickpea salad

*T*HOUGH chickpeas were once said in the South of France to be a dish for the poor, this salad now has its place on the best tables.

You will need dried chickpeas, bicarbonate of soda, salt, a small bowl of well-seasoned French dressing, a few spring onions (called « cébettes » in the South of France), and some parsley.

Soak the chickpeas in cold water for a whole night, then rinse them out. Cook in cold water which will then be put to the boil for about an hour and a half. Add one pinch of bicarbonate of soda and another of salt.

Drain, and add the French dressing, the chopped spring onions and the parsley. Serve warm.

Canned chickpeas are as good as dried ones. You can place them in boiling water for a few minutes before dressing and serving.

Salade fère ou salade sauvage

Wild salad

*T*HIS recipe should ideally begin by an early walk in the woods, gathering herbs with a small knife and a basket.

The herbs should be a mix of dandelions, wild lettuce, endive, purslane "Rocket" and any edible herb with a strong flavour. A salad of this sort requires a good knowledge of plants, or a good friend who knows about them, but its savours are incomparable.

This salad is close to the blending called « mesclun » in the South of France, which can be found in shops ready to serve, but it must be seasoned carefully so as to keep the subtlety of its flavours : a dressing made of olive oil, salt, lemon juice and a little garlic is fine.

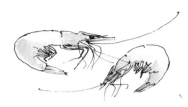

Salade camarguaise

T is high time we rediscovered the rice from Camargue, which is as good as its American cousins.

Cook one cup of white rice from Camargue for each guest, Creole fashion (place the rice in a saucepan, covering it with cold water, with a knob of butter and a pinch of salt, and bring it to the boil. Cover and simmer for ten to twelve minutes until the water is absorbed.) You will also need one head of celery, some flat parsley, fresh shrimps or small squids and a dressing made of olive oil and lemon.

Prepare the dressing in a salad bowl with ground pepper, and, if you like their flavour, a few mustard seeds.

Wash the celery head and cut it into fine pieces. Place them in a bowl.

Cook the shrimps in court-bouillon, and peel when lukewarm.

Alternatively, cut up the squids and cook them in a frying pan for a quarter of an hour so that they release their water, adding olive oil when almost cooked.

Mix the rice with the sauce, and garnish with the sea-food and with a few leaves of parsley.

Caviar d'aubergines

Aubergine/Eggplant "caviar"

*T*HIS caviar has to be prepared beforehand and served very cold, on toasted bread or with raw vegetables.

Take 4 plump aubergines/eggplants, a few chopped spring onions, and any herbs you like : parsley for instance, or basil, thyme or savory. You will also need some olive oil.

Split the aubergines into two and cook them in a hot oven for half an hour. Remove the pulp with a tablespoon and grind using a ricer.

Incorporate the chopped herbs and onions into the «caviar» and add a dash of olive oil to obtain a creamy consistency.

Caillettes provençales

OR 6 caillettes, take some caul («crépine» in French), a slice of lard, 250 g/9 oz of pork's liver, and 250 g/9 oz of chine.

You will also need one pound of spinach, ten crushed juniper berries, one egg, some salt and pepper and a glass of white wine.

Soak the caul in cold water while you prepare the stuffing.

Clean the spinach, blanch and strain. Finely chop the chine, the liver and the lard. Mix in a salad bowl with the strained chopped spinach.

Add the egg, the juniper berries, the salt and pepper.
Share the stuffing into six balls and shut each of them into a square of caul.
Place the caillettes into an oven dish and pour the wine over them.
Put in a medium oven for about 45 minutes.
The caillettes are served either warm or cold.

Pissaladière

Onion tart

*F*OR *the pastry, you will need a large bowl of plain flour, two heaped tablespoons of butter and olive oil, one pinch of salt and a little warm water. Also take 3 or 4 onions, a few anchovies, and a few black olives.*

Pour the flour into the salad bowl, and add the butter, cut into small pieces, as well as the oil and the salt.

Pour just enough warm water to soften up the butter, and to obtain an elastic pastry. Allow to rest for half an hour.

Meanwhile, clean the onions, chop them finely and sweat them gently in a little olive oil until they are translucent, but not yet brown.

Spread the pastry onto an oiled tart dish. Place the cooked onions over it, as well as the olives and the anchovies on top.

Place the *pissaladière* in a medium oven for thirty minutes.

It can be served either warm or cold.

Papeton d'aubergines

*T*HIS is said to have been the favourite dish of the popes in Avignon, hence the name of this delicate and distinguished starter.

Take one kg/2 lb of aubergines/eggplants, 1 tablespoon of cooking salt, 2 garlic cloves, one onion, 3 eggs, 1 dl of cream, a little olive oil, some thyme and pepper.

Clean the aubergines, cut them into squares and sweat them with salt for an hour – throw away their water, then heat the oil and throw the eggplants in it, along with the garlic and the onion. Add pepper and thyme. Cook gently for half an hour, stirring frequently – put it through the ricer. Add the whipped eggs and cream. Place in a buttered casserole dish in a hot oven in a bain-marie for half an hour.

Serve warm or cold with a «coulis de tomates». (See page 20.)

Fougasse aux olives

VERY typical, the small salted fougasse are served as a starter, an appetizer or a snack.

To make 4 small olive fougasses, take 500 g/1 lb of flour, 20 g/1 oz of fresh yeast, 4 tablespoons of olive oil, 1 tablespoons of sugar, one pinch of salt, and a bowl of olives, without the stones.

Mix the yeast into some warm water. Pour the flour into a salad bowl and, in the middle, pour the oil, the sugar, the salt and the yeast, and enough warm water to get a supple pastry.

Knead on a floured board until the pastry does not stick to your fingers anymore.

Cover with a clean cloth, and leave to rise in a warm place for one or two hours.

Knead the pastry once more, this time adding the olives.

Divide it into four equal parts and flatten them. Make a few slots in each fougassette and enlarge them with the hand. Place them on a buttered and floured baking-tray. Cover with a cloth, and allow to rise once again. Glaze with 1 egg-yolk or with milk.

Cook for twenty-five minutes in a quick oven.

CHAPTER 3

Soups

*P*ICTURE this : In the kitchen, the door ajar, the cooking-pot is see-thing. The white tureen is brought, still streaming to the polished table. In the plates are some hot bread croutons.

- *Aïgo boulido,*
- *Soupe de pois chiches,* Chickpeas soup
- *Soupe au pistou,* Pesto soup
- *Soupe d'épeautre,* Spelt soup
- *Soupe de poissons,* Fish soup
- *Soupe aux moules,* Mussel soup.

Aigo boulido

*T*HE most simple of all soups, as its name suggests : boiled water.

For three or four guests, take three or four garlic cloves, one litre of water, one bay leaf and some sage. A little salt is enough.

Cook all the ingredients except the sage for 15 minutes. Turn the heat off, add the sage and cover.
Meanwhile, place slices of bread fried in olive oil and covered with grated cheese on the plates.
Pour the bouillon over them.

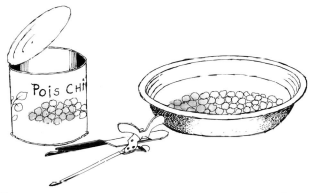

Soupe de pois chiches

Chickpeas soup

*T*HIS recipe has to be planned a day beforehand to leave time for the chickpeas to soak, if they are dried.

Take some chickpeas, the white parts of two leeks, 2 tomatoes, 2 garlic cloves, salt and pepper, and some olive oil and bread for the croutons. Soak and then cook the chickpeas according to the recipe on page 27, without straining them.

Meanwhile, in a casserole dish, sweat the chopped leek and then the tomatoes and the garlic. Add salt and pepper and simmer for 15 minutes, blending the cooked chickpeas and their water. Cook for a few minutes more, then strain the soup.

Serve on hot croutons.

Soupe au pistou

Pesto soup

*B*RING *home from the market one pound of green beans, 2 cour-gettes/zucchinis, 3 tomatoes, 3 potatoes, a handful of haricot beans, and kidney beans, some vermicelli and some salt.*

For the pesto, add the ingredients indicated on page 17.

Cook the haricot beans and the kidney beans in two litres of water or more. Add little by little, the other fresh vegetables, chopped into squares, then add salt. Cook for at least an hour, then add the vermicelli. Cook for 15 more minutes.

Meanwhile, prepare the pesto, then pour it in the soup before serving or present it in a jar so that every guests can help himself.

Soupe d'épeautre
Spelt soup

*T*HE spelt («épeautre»), looks like wheat. It is easily found in Provence.

For a large soup, you will need the bone of a lamb's leg, one bowl of spelt, one onion with two cloves in it, one leek, two carrots and one rind sausage named « missoun » in Provence. You may also add three sticks of celery and one turnip without, of course, forgetting the salt.

Cook the bone, the roughly chopped vegetables and the spelt in 3 litres of water. Add the sausage, pricked with a fork, when the soup is half cooked.

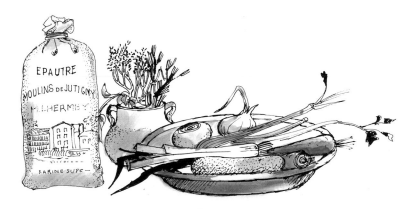

Soupe de poissons

Fish soup

*F*ISH *out at sea, on the port or to your favourite fish merchant, 1 kg/2 lb of various saltwater fishes. Take 2 onions, 3 tomatoes, some fennel, a little thyme, 1 bay leaf, 2 garlic cloves, a pinch of safran, some salt and a little olive oil.*

Scale and gut the fishes, chop them into pieces, then brown them into the olive oil with onion, cut into slivers.

Add the tomatoes, the garlic and the seasoning.

Cover with water and simmer for fifteen minutes.

Sieve, reheat and serve boiling with *rouille* (page 19) and croutons.

Soupe aux moules

Mussel soup

AKE one kilogram/2lb of mussels, 2 bay leaves, the white part of a leek, 1 onion, some olive oil, one pinch of safran and some parsley. You will also need either a bowl of raw rice or Vermicelli, or 2 or 3 potatoes, cleaned and cut into squares.

Open the cleaned and brushed mussels in boiling water, with the bay leaf.
Remove the shells and filter their juice in a square of muslin.
Meanwhile, brown the leek and the chopped onions in the olive oil.
Pour the juice over it and bring to the boil adding, if necessary, water or white wine.
Add the safran and the rice, vermicelli, or potatoes. Simmer for twenty minutes and then, just before serving, add the mussels and the minced parsley.

CHAPTER 4

Fish and sea-food from the Mediterranean

*T*HE sound of waves is so soft, here, that it cannot be heard ten steps away but the sails flap loudly against the masts.

On a large piece of cork bark, by way of a dish, the catch of the day is spread : sea urchins, mullet, and a big octopus.

When you take them home to cook, the kitchen will be full of sea air.

- *Rougets poêlés,* Fried mullets
- *Loup au fenouil,* Bass with fennel
- *La bouillabaisse,*
- *Brandade,* Cod brandade
- *Raïté de morue,* Cod stew
- *Tian de sardines,* Sardines and spinach au gratin
- *Sardines en escabèche,* Marinated sardines
- *Poulpe à la provençale,* Octopus à la Provençale
- *Pilau de moules.*

FARINE

Rougets poêlés
Red mullets

*Y*OU will need 2 red mullets for each guest.

Gut the fishes, without scaling them, and cook them in a little olive oil in a hot frying-pan, like a beefsteak. Add salt and pepper.

The skin should stick to the scales; only the flesh is eaten.

Do not throw the heads away, as the cheeks are considered to be the best part.

Alternatively, scale the fish and roll them into flour before cooking them if you wish to eat the skin.

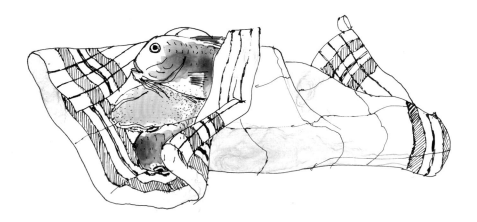

Loup au fenouil

Bass with fennel

THE bass can be cooked either in the oven or on a barbecue. Depending on how big the fish is, it will feed two to four guests.

For each bass, use one handful of fresh fennel.

After gutting the fish stuff it with fennel. Cut the skin, add salt and pepper, and cook on the barbecue, or in the oven, on a dish to which has been added a glass of white wine or pastis with water.

Cooking time will of course depend on the weight of the fish.

La bouillabaisse

*I*F traditionally, the bouillabaisse was a dish for the poor, nowadays, however, it is served on festive occasions. But first of all, it has to be prepared by men! They will preferably cook it on a wood fire, in a huge cooking-pot.

Buy or fish a nice variety of scorpion fish («rascasses»), rainbow wrass («galinette»), girella («girelles»), conger («congre»), monkfish («lotte»), dory («saint-Pierre»), as well as a few crabs, big winkles, according to the fresh catch.

Take enough potatoes for everyone, two big onions cut into four pieces, Three or four tomatoes roughly chopped, a few garlic cloves, some fennel, the peel of an orange, some salt and pepper, some safran and a little olive oil.

Prepare a *rouille* (see page 19).

In the cooking-pot, quickly brown in olive oil the onions, the potatoes, the spices, the tomatoes and the condiments, and stir well.

Then, place the crabs and the firmer fishes, and on top of those, the most tender, such as monkfish, for instance.

Cover with boiling water and cook for fifteen minutes on a brisk heat.

Carefully place the fish on a dish with the potatoes, and serve the bouillon separately with toasted bread and rouille.

Brandade de morue
Cod brandade

*Y*OU can easily find this speciality from Nîmes ready-made, but of course, an home-made brandade is always best.

Remember you'll have to soak the brandade for twenty-four hours in cold water. Take 1 kg/2 lb of cod, some fresh milk and a little olive oil.

Once the cod has soaked for 24 hours, blanch it: place it in a saucepan filled with cold water, heat until it begins to boil, turn the heat off, cover and leave to stand for ten minutes. Split up the cod into small pieces, and remove the bones, but leave the skin.

Place the cod in a saucepan and heat. Stir while pouring little by little the olive oil, and the warm milk until you obtain a pommade.

Serve with potatoes, croutons, and toasted bread.

Raïté de morue

Cod stew

AKE 1 kg/2 lb of soaked cod, some olive oil, 2 small onions, 1,5 glass of red wine, 1,5 glass of water, 2 garlic cloves, 1 blending of aromatic herbs, some salt and pepper, 2 tablespoons of plain flour, 2 tablespoons of tomato puree, and 2 tablespoons of capers.

Sweat the onion in a little olive oil, and add the flour. Water down with the wine, and the water add the crushed garlic, and the aromatic herbs, the salt and pepper, and mix the sauce with the tomato puree.

Leave to simmer for twenty minutes.

Meanwhile, cut the cot into pieces, roll them into he flour, and fry them for a few minutes. Throw the pieces in the sauce, add the capers, and allow to simmer a little more before serving.

Tian de sardines

Sardines and spinach au gratin

TAKE 3 or 4 sardines for each guest, 1 kg/2 lb of spinach or chard, 1 egg, a little olive oil, and breadcrumbs.

Clean and blanch the spinach in a little salted water, and drain well.

Scale the sardines and clean them out, cutting off the heads. Then open them up, and remove the central bone.

Oil an oven dish and fill it with the chopped spinach mixed with the egg. Then place the sardines in the dish, their skin on top, season, water with olive oil, and sprinkle with breadcrumbs.

Brown in a hot oven for 10 minutes.

Sardines en escabèche

Marinated sardines

TAKE 1 kg/2 lb of sardines, 1 little flour, 2 carrots, 1 stick of celery, 1 onion, 1 chilli, a few corns of black pepper and a few juniper berries, a few bay leaves, 1 bowl of wine vinegar, and a little olive oil.

Scale and clean out the sardines, and remove their heads. Open them so as to remove the central bone. Dry the sardines, roll them in a little flour and fry them quickly in a pan.

Strain them on kitchen paper, and place them in a terrine.

Brown the sliced vegetables in a little olive oil. Remove the terrine from the heat, and add the spices and the vinegar. Heat again until the vinegar boils, and pour this marinade over the sardines.

Refrigerate and serve two days later.

Poulpe à la provençale

Octopus à la Provençale

CUTTLEFISH or squid will do as well for this recipe, and in this case, you won't need to tenderize the two cephalopods!

Tenderize 1 kg/2 lb of octopus by beating it with a stick. Clean and cut it into pieces. Also take 3 tomatoes, 1 garlic clove, 2 onions, 1 glass of "coulis de tomate" (see page 20), 1 piece of orange peel, fennel, and a little olive oil.

In a large casserole dish, brown the pieces of octopus, and the chopped onions. Add the roughly chopped tomatoes, the coulis, the garlic, and the orange peel. Stir well. Put the fennel on top and cover.

Cook for 20 minutes for the squids, or one hour for the octopus, adding a little water or white wine if the sauce has reduced too much.

Remove the fennel before serving.

Pilau de moules

*T*AKE *2 litres of mussels, 2 glasses of raw rice, 1 onion, 1 tomato, 1 pinch of safran, a little olive oil, some salt and pepper, and a "bouquet garni".*

Clean the mussels and heat them for a few minutes in a large saucepan to open them.

Remove the shells (except a few to decorate), and filter the juice through a square of muslin. Brown the chopped onion in a little olive oil, and add the tomato, and the raw rice. Stir until the rice browns.

Pour 5 glasses of a liquid made of the mussels'juice and water over the rice, cover and cook on a very slow heat for 20 minutes.

CHAPTER 5

Spring dishes

In spring, on the hills of Provence, the fresh herbs peep out among the flowers, and Provence is for a very short time verdant.

This is the time to glean the spring vegetables in the market or the garden and to pick up wild herbs during early morning walks.

During the Easter season, it is also a good time for lamb, and eggs.

- *Brouillade de pointes d'asperges,*
    Scrambled eggs with asparagus tips
- *Omelette au vert,* Green omelette
- *Crespéou,*
- *Barbouillade d'artichauts,*
- *Artichauts farcis,* Stuffed artichokes
- *Épaule d'agneau en garrigue,*
    Shoulder of lamb with aromatic herbs
- *Sauté d'agneau aux légumes de printemps,*
    Sauté of lamb with spring vegetables
- *Ravioles au fromage de chèvre,*
    Ravioles with goats'cheese.

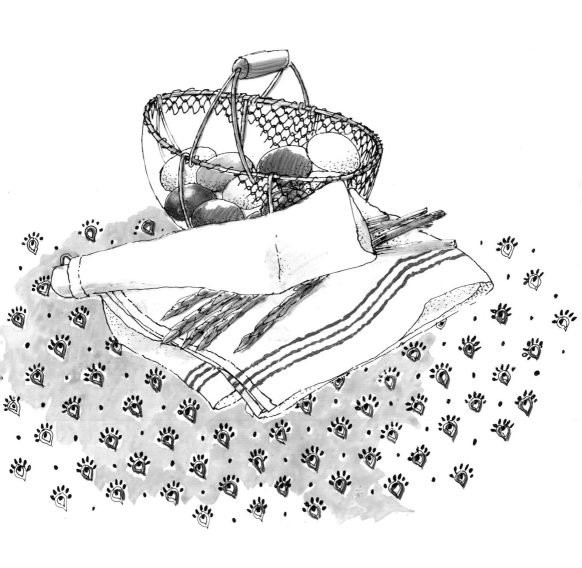

Brouillade de pointes d'asperges

Scrambled eggs with asparagus tips

*T*HIS dish is delicious with the fine wild green asparagus that can be found by the paths of Provence. It will be equally a success with fresh asparagus from the market.

Take 6 small asparagus and 2 eggs per guest.

Cut the higher parts of the asparagus. Rinse out in fresh water and brown quickly in a frying pan. Place the asparagus in a clay dish, on a slow heat, and break the eggs, stirring all the time.

Season with salt and pepper and do not overcook (the brouillade has to be moist)

The brouillade can be eaten as a smooth cream spread on bread or with some lettuce.

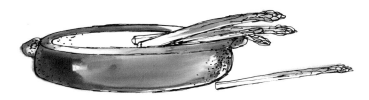

Omelette au vert

Green omelette

YOU will need a handful of baby spinach and as many herbs as you like : parsley, or, chives, etc, a clove of garlic and some olive oil, and two eggs per guest.

Brown the chopped spinach and the aromatic herbs and add the crushed garlic.

Whip the eggs and pour them in the frying pan. Cook the omelette and serve it runny.

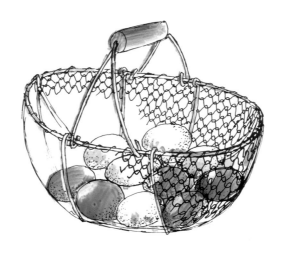

Crespéou

*T*HE *crespéou* is a cake made of omelettes placed on top of each other.

You will need a dozen eggs and three tablespoons of milk and different ingredients for each omelette: one red pepper, one green pepper, four spring onions, three artichoke hearts, or, according to your taste: tomatoes, aubergines/eggplants, courgettes/zucchinis, ham, tapenade, etc.

Whip the eggs with the milk and then season them.

In a medium frying pan, brown one chopped pepper in olive oil and pour over it one ladle full of whipped eggs to make the first omelette. It must be thin and runny. Place it in a dish and make another one with another vegetable, alternating the colours. As for the artichoke hearts, which need to be cooked for a longer time, it might be easier to cook them beforehand.

The crespéou should be eaten cold the day after you have cooked it, cut in slices like a big cake, and should be served with a salad.

Barbouillade d'artichauts

*B*UY *a few young and tender artichokes, one or two per guest. You will also need a slice of salted pork* (petit salé) *cut into lardons, one onion, a glass of white wine, some thyme, olive oil, and lemon, salt and pepper.*

Pull out the external leaves of the artichokes and cut the top part of the others. Cut each artichoke into two pieces, and remove the choke. Cut each piece into four other pieces, and place them in a little water, with the lemon juice.

Brown the lardons in a casserole dish with a little olive oil and the minced onion. Add the artichokes, some salt, pepper and thyme. After it has browned, add with the white wine. Leave to cook on a slow heat for twenty or thirty minutes.

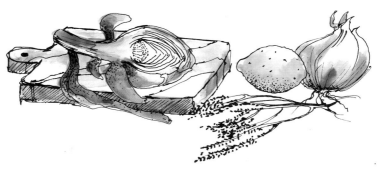

Artichauts farcis

Stuffed artichokes

*F*OR *each guest, you will need two small purple artichokes and four thin slices of streaky bacon. For the stuffing, you will need the soft part of a loaf, soaked in milk, some garlic, parsley, salt, pepper and an egg yolk. You will also need two carrots, one onion and a little olive oil.*

Prepare the artichokes as in the last recipe. Cut them into two and remove the choke. Throw them into the water and lemon. Peel and finely slice the onion and the carrot and brown them slowly with a little olive oil in a casserole dish. Season with salt and pepper, and stir well so that it doesn't stick.

Prepare the stuffing by mixing the ingredients mentioned above and fill each half artichoke with it. Wrap a slice of streaky bacon around each of them and tie with a piece of string.

Place the artichokes in a casserole with a little water and leave to simmer for 3 quarters of an hour.

Epaule d'agneau en garrigue

Shoulder of lamb with aromatic herbs

To prepare one shoulder of lamb, gather the following herbs and condiments in a large dish : thyme, rosemary, ground savory (it is important that it should be ground, as savory is sharp)*, crushed peppercorns and juniper berries, some cooking salt, and a few bread crumbs.*

Make an incision at the shoulder along the bone and slip part of the mixture of herbs in the meat.

Tie up the shoulder, brush it with olive oil and roll it in the rest of herbs. Cook it in a hot oven like a leg of lamb, for a quarter of an hour per pound. Serve it with beans, or some small potatoes cooked in the oven with the lamb.

Sauté d'agneau aux légumes de printemps

Sauté of lamb with spring vegetables

TAKE 1 kg/2 lb of lamb sauté, 2 onions, 3 spring carrots, 1 big tomato, 1 bowl of peas, some spring onions, garlic, olive oil, thyme, rosemary, salt and pepper.

Brown the pieces of meat with the onion and some olive oil in a casserole dish.

Add the sliced carrots, 4 garlic cloves in their skin, the aromatic herbs and the tomato. Season, cover and simmer for forty-five minutes, adding water or white wine if need be.

Add the chopped peas, and spring onions, and let fifteen more minutes on the fire.

Ravioles au fromage de chèvre

Ravioles with goats'cheese

*T*HEY take a while to prepare, and ask a little attention, but the home-made ravioles are very tasty.

For 8 dozen big ravioles, take 1 pound of flour, and 4 eggs, and – for the stuffing – 1 pound of fresh spinach and 2 very fresh goats'cheese.

Pour the flour into a mixing bowl. Break the eggs and add a pinch of salt and just enough water to get a consistent dough. Don't knead it too much. Cover it with a cloth and leave for half an hour.

Meanwhile, blanch the spinach in a little salted water. Strain well and squeeze it in your hands. Mix with the goats'cheeses and season.

Split the dough into four parts. Roll out each part on a floured piece of wood. With a ruler, mark out squares of about 3 cm. Place a knob of stuffing in the middle of each square. Cover with another piece of rolled out dough, and press the ruler again firmly on the square patterns, so as to join the two layers.

Cut the squares with a pastry wheel, or with a knife.

Do the same with the two other parts of dough.

Flour the ravioles well so that they don't stick together and cook them in a lot of salted water for five minutes.

Strain and serve hot with a dash of olive oil and some grated cheese.

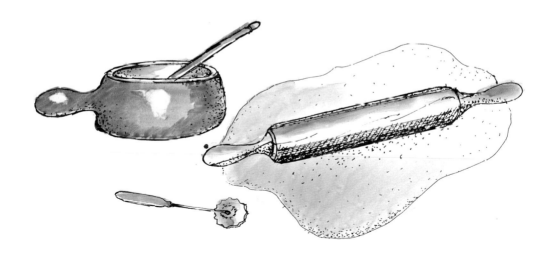

CHAPTER 6
Summer dishes

*T*N the warm, still air, the cicadas sing loud. The baskets, after the market, are heavy with plump fruits bursting with sunshine. The scent of crushed basil mixes with the fragrance of the lavender bushes. It is noon, in full sunlight, and Provence is more provencal than ever. This is our summer.

- *Tomates provençales,* Provencal tomatoes
- *Tian de courgettes,* Courgettes au gratin
- *Beignets de fleurs de courgettes,*
    Courgette/zucchini blossom friters
- *Flan de courgettes,* Courgettes/zucchinis custard pie
- *Gratin d'aubergines,* Aubergines/eggplants au gratin
- *Daube d'aubergines,* Stewed aubergines/eggplants
- *Ratatouille,* Vegetable stew
- *Farcis de Provence,* Stuffed vegetables
- *Poulet d'ail,* Chicken stuffed with garlic
- *Canard aux figues,* Duck with figs
- *Pâtes au pistou,* Pasta and pesto
- *Pan bagna.*

Tomates provençales

Provencal tomatoes

*T*HIS is a classic in Provence, very simple and delicious as long as you don't rush the cooking time.

Take 1 big tomato per guest, 2 or 3 cloves of garlic, some salt and pepper, parsley, a few bread crumbs, and some olive oil.

Divide the tomatoes in two and seed them. In a large frying pan, place them in some olive oil on the side of the cut, and cook on a slow heat.

Turn them over when they have released their water, season and let to cook slowly for up to an hour. Ten minutes before the end of the cooking, sprinkle with chopped parsley and garlic, and then some bread crumbs.

The tomatoes can equally be served with meat or rice.

Tian de courgettes

Courgettes au gratin

*F*ROM this dish, you can make many variations by mixing the courgettes with any other vegetable.

For each guest, take 1 courgette/zucchini, some salt, pepper, nutmeg, a little flour, some olive oil, and a little grated cheese.

Without peeling them, finely slice the courgettes and roll them quickly in a little flour. Brown them with olive oil, season and pour into an oil thick oven proof dish. Cover with grated cheese and brown in the oven.

Beignets de fleurs de courgettes

Courgette/zucchini blossom friters

WHEN there are plenty of courgettes/zucchinis growing wild, take a few blossoms. They are also found in the market place sometimes.

Apart from the flowers, take, for the batter 200 g/7 oz of flour, 2 eggs, 1 glass of milk, 1 pinch of salt, and 1 of baking soda as well as some frying oil.

Prepare the batter by mixing the above ingredients in a salad bowl and rest for half an hour. Remove the blossoms stalks, then wash and dry them. Dip the blossoms one after the other in the batter and fry them.

You might like to cook stick of courgettes or other vegetables according to the same recipe.

Flan de courgettes

Courgettes/zucchinis custard pie

TAKE 1 kg/2 lb of courgettes/zucchinis, 4 eggs, 1 glass of milk, 2 crushed cloves of garlic, some chopped chives, a few chopped basil leaves, some salt and pepper and some grated cheese.

Without peeling them, cut the courgettes into sections, and steam. Crush them with a pestle or a fork, and strain if need be.

Mix with the other ingredients, pour into an oiled oven-proof dish and cook for 30 minutes in a hot oven.

This «flan» can be served either hot or warm.

Gratin d'aubergines

Aubergines/eggplants au gratin…

TAKE 2 big aubergines, 2 tomatoes, and 2 onions, 1 clove of garlic, some Parmesan cheese, some bread crumbs, some olive oil, salt and pepper.

Without peeling them, cut lengthwise thin slices of aubergine and brown them with olive oil, in a casserole dish. Add the sliced onion, then the tomatoes and the pounded garlic. Season, cover, and simmer for 45 minutes.

In an oiled oven-proof dish, alternate the layers of vegetables with layers of Parmesan cheese and top off with the bread crumbs.

Daube d'aubergines

Stewed aubergines/eggplants

TAKE 1 kg/2 lb of aubergines/eggplants, 1 pound of tomatoes, 1 onion, 1 stick of celery, 1 slice of salted pork ("petit salé"), a few cloves of garlic, some olive oil, thyme and pepper.

In a casserole dish, brown the sliced onion and the chopped pork. Add the chopped tomatoes, allowing them to release their juices.

Then, dice and add the unpeeled aubergines, the chopped celery and at last the crushed garlic.

Season, cover, and let to simmer, stirring from time to time so that the vegetables don't stick.

La ratatouille

Vegetable stew

T is also called "Bohémienne", although nobody agrees on whether or not there is a difference between the two dishes. It is the summer dish in Provence par excellence blending all its best products.

Take 1 pound of aubergines/eggplants, 1 pound of courgettes/zucchinis, 2 peppers, 2 onions and 2 pounds of tomatoes, as well as some thyme, a few garlic cloves, some pepper and some olive oil.

Dice the unpeeled aubergines and courgettes, and slice the onions, the peppers and the tomatoes. Heat the oil in a casserole dish and add the vegetables, browning them one at a time.

Begin with the aubergines, then add the peppers, the onions, the courgettes and finally, the tomatoes. Add the crushed garlic, season and simmer for about 45 minutes. The ratatouille is best served with any grilled meat or fish, and with rice or pasta as well.

As a starter, it is often served cold with a dash of olive oil, and a leaf of mint for those who like it.

Farcis de Provence

Stuffed vegetables

*S*TUFFED vegetables, a long-standing tradition in Provence, are as tasty as they look.

Take, choosing among tomatoes, aubergines/eggplants, courgettes/zucchinis, peppers, fennel and onions, a few vegetables of the same size.

As for the stuffing, take 1 small bowl of cooked rice, 1 small bowl minced meat (left-overs, sausage meat…), *1 egg, some Parmesan cheese, aromatic herbs, such as parsley, chives or tarragon.*

Blanch the onions for a few minutes, and then for all the vegetables, cut the higher part, so as to form a lid.

Empty the pulp of each vegetable, and keep, except for the seeds of the peppers. Place the vegetables in an oiled oven – proof dish and make the stuffing. Brown the minced meat in a frying pan and add the vegetables pulp, finely chopped.

Take it away from the fire, and mix with the rice, the egg, the Parmesan cheese and the chopped herbs, and season. Fill the vegetables with the stuffing, replace the lids on top and cook in the oven for about one hour.

Poulet d'ail

Chicken stuffed with garlic

*T*HIS recipe is very simple. It is also delicious, though it might seem a little surprising at first.

Take 1 big chicken and about 40 garlic cloves, some salt and pepper and a little olive oil.

Flambé the gutted chicken, then season the inside with salt and pepper and fill it with the garlic cloves in their skin.

Close the chicken with toothpicks or string, brush it with olive oil, salt and pepper and cook in the oven for about an hour and a half.

Then, prepare some croutons to spread over the melted garlic (see *ail en chemise*, page 23).

Canard aux figues

Duck with figs

TAKE 1 duck, 1 pound of figs, 1 slice of salted pork, 1 glass of white wine and some salt and pepper.

Finely chop the salted pork and mix it with half of the roughly chopped figs. Season well, and stuff the duck with it.

Place the duck in a oven-proof dish, with the rest of the figs around it. Add the wine, season once again and cook in the oven for an hour or more, according to the duck size.

Pâtes au pistou

Pasta and pesto

THE best pasta for this recipe is wide and flat, like tagliatelle. Better still: you can make your own pasta by using the dough used for the ravioles on page 66.

As for the pesto, you should follow the recipe on page 17, but you might like to add a little double cream on it.

Served the pasta cooked *"al dente"* boiling hot, directly on the plates, with a tablespoon of sauce in the middle and a few leaves of fresh basil.

Pan bagna

THIS recipe, served with a fresh salad, will make a perfect rustic lunch, or a ready meal for a picnic.

For each guest, take 1 small round loaf, some garlic and olive oil, 2 anchovies, 1 small sliced tomato, 1/2 a hard boiled egg, some tuna and a few stoned black olives.

Cut the higher part of the bread to form a lid, and remove most of its white part. Rub its inside with a clove of garlic and pour a dash of olive oil over it. Place the other ingredients in it and close.

CHAPTER 7

Autumn dishes

*T*HE pathways smell of undergrowth, moss and dead leaves. We are on the look out for the first mushrooms, like the noble cep, and all the others too, horns of plenty or club moss. At the end of the season, we may pick the olives either green or ripe

- *Terrine de champignons en croûte,*
  Mushrooms en croûte
- *Canard aux olives,* Duck with olives
- *Pâtes aux olives,* Pasta with olives
- *Lapin à la pèbre d'ail,* Rabbit and savory
- *Pâtes aux cèpes,* Pasta with ceps
- *Cailles en feuille de vigne,* Quails in vine leaves
- *Rissoles,* Turnovers
- *Tourte au potiron,* Pumpkin pie.

Terrine de champignons en croûte
Mushrooms en croûte

*T*RY this recipe with any mushrooms you like, mixed or not, as long as they are edible! This dish has to be cooked beforehand, the day before for example, so that it is really cold when served.

Take 1 pound of cleaned mushrooms, all hard and dirty parts removed, 2 pounded cloves of garlic and some olive oil. You will also need 1/4 of French bread, some milk, 2 eggs, 1 bowl of minced meat (half sausage meat, half left-overs, veal, or anything you like), 2 slices of streaky bacon (a thin one and the other diced), 1 handful of raw spinach, a few juniper berries, some salt and pepper. For the pastry, you will need some plain flour, butter, and olive oil.

Prepare the pastry according to the "pissaladière" recipe on page 33, and leave to stand.

Meanwhile, in a large mixing bowl, leave the crushed bread to soak in the milk.

Brown the mushrooms in a frying-pan with some olive oil and the garlic. Mince one third of the mushrooms and keep the rest.

Squeeze the bread in your hands and throw away the rest of milk.
Add, in the salad bowl, the eggs, the meat, and the diced bacon, the minced mushrooms, the finely chopped spinach, one dozen pounded juniper berries, some salt and pepper. Stir well.

Roll out the pastry and cover a buttered terrine with it. Pour over the pastry half the stuffing, one layer of mushrooms, the rest of the stuffing, and another layer of mushrooms. Finish with the thin slice of bacon. Cover the terrine with a lid made of pastry and cut 4 diamond-shaped holes so that the stream comes out.

Decorate with the rest of the pastry and a few juniper berries, brush with some milk and cook in the oven for an hour and a half, in a bain-marie (placing your terrine in another recipient with a little water at the bottom).

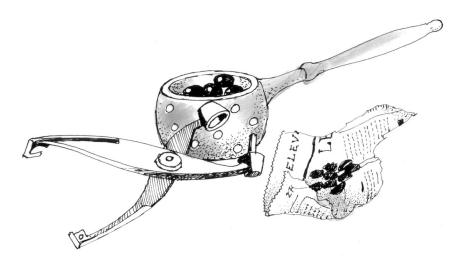

Canard aux olives

Duck with olives

*T*AKE *1 small duck, 1 bowl of black olives, 1 non-treated lemon, 1 glass of white wine, some salt and pepper.*

Cut up the duck and brown it with olive oil in a casserole dish. Stone the olives and add them to the duck.

Thinly slice the unpeeled lemon and drop it in the casserole dish. When the meat is browned, add the white wine, season, and then cover and leave to simmer for about one hour.

Pâtes aux olives

Pasta with olives

*F*OR *this recipe, take any small sort of pasta, and some "olives cassées". (They're olives which have been broken when gathered so as to enhance their flavour. However, they can prove very difficult to find anywhere other than in Provence. As an alternative, use plain black olives.) Also take a few cloves of garlic, and some olive oil.*

Stone roughly one bowl of olives, and cook the pasta in a large saucepan of salted water.

Meanwhile, brown the olives in a frying-pan, with a few tablespoons of olive oil and two to three crushed garlic cloves.

When the pasta is « al dente », strain and pour into the frying-pan. Stir and serve.

This dish can be prepared beforehand and then reheated.

Lapin à la pèbre d'aï
Rabbit and savory

*T*HE *pèbre d'ail* is a nice name for savory, an aromatic herb that is delicious with rabbit.

Take 1 rabbit, chopped into pieces, with its liver and kidneys, some olive oil, some savory, fresh if possible, 1 small tomato, 2 garlic cloves, 1 dash of vinegar, some salt and pepper.

Brown the pieces of rabbit with some olive oil in a casserole dish. Season, then add the savory, and the tomato, cut into two. Leave to cook on a slow fire for about an hour.

Place the pieces of rabbit in a dish and keep warm, then remove both tomato and savory.

Mince the liver and the kidneys, crush the garlic and put in the casserole dish on a quick heat and pound well, adding a dash of vinegar and serving this sauce boiling hot with the rabbit.

Pâtes aux cèpes

Pasta with ceps

ACCORDING to the ceps size, take about 1 for each guest, some garlic, some olive oil and parsley, as well as pasta, tagliatelle or spaghetti for instance.

Brush the ceps so as to remove all the dirt and keep the nicest parts of the hats apart. Mince the rest thinly and crush the garlic.

While the pasta is cooking, brown, in two different frying-pans the minced mushrooms and garlic, and the sliced hats. Season and sprinkle with the thinly chopped parsley.

Serve the strained pasta on each plate, with a tablespoon of the sauce, and a few slices of cep and a dash of olive oil.

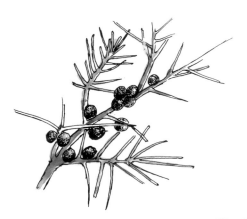

Cailles en feuille de vigne

Quails in vine leaves

*T*HE quails can easily be hunted down in any supermarket, but they might be finer if procured at a poulterer's or from an impenitent hunter. Thrushes and other small birds can also be prepared according to this recipe.

Take 1 or 2 quails for each guest, and as many nice vine leaves and thin slices of streaky bacon. For the stuffing, take the livers of the quails, 3 juniper berries for each bird, some thinly larded bacon, some chopped shallots, and some salt and pepper.

You'll also need 1 glass of white wine, some slices of bread, some garlic and some olive oil.

Prepare the stuffing by mixing the chopped liver, the shallots, the larded bacon and the crushed juniper berries. Season.

Flambé the quails and stuff them. Then, roll them first in a vine leaf and then in a slice of bacon, and tie with some string.

Brown the birds in a casserole dish with a few tablespoons of olive oil, then pour the wine over them, cover and leave to cook for twenty to thirty minutes.

Brown a few slices of bread rubbed with garlic and then serve each quail on a slice of bread.

Rissoles
Turnovers

*T*HIS recipe is perfect for left-overs, either meat or vegetables, and can be served with a fresh green salad.

Take some ready-made puff pastry and some frying oil. For the stuffing, take any left-overs of meat, vegetables, mushrooms, 1 egg, a few spring onions or white onions, some parsley, salt and pepper.

In a salad-bowl, mix all the thinly chopped ingredients. Roll out the puff pastry and cut it into circles with a large glass or a small bowl (about 7 cm in diameter).

Place a tablespoon of stuffing on half of each circle and close like a turnover, wetting the edges to join them. Fry for a few minutes on each side and strain on kitchen paper before serving.

Tourte au potiron
Pumpkin pie

*T*AKE *1 kg/2 lb of pumpkin pulp, 1 onion, 3 eggs, some grated cheese, 1 nutmeg, some salt and pepper and, for the pastry, some flour butter and olive oil.*

Prepare a shortcrust pastry according to the recipe of the **"pissaladière"** on page 33 and leave to stand.

Peel the pumpkin and dice it. Cook it with very little salted water and the chopped onion until it is tender.

Strain, mash the pulp with a fork, mix it with the eggs and the grated cheese, and season.

Roll out the pastry, keeping one third of it and line a buttered tin with it. Fill the tin with the pumpkin, decorate with intersected pieces of pastry and cook for about forty minutes on a medium heat.

CHAPTER 8

Winter dishes

*I*N the large fireplaces, the vine shoots are burning. The *"santons"* (figures put in the crib for Christmas) are about to be let out of the cupboard to celebrate Christmas and its dinner, the *"gros souper"*. In the garden, we gather oranges and mimosa.

We know that the winter is not long here. There's just enough time to enjoy the festivities.

> – *La daube,* Beef stew,
> – *Macaronade,* Macaroni au gratin,
> – *Rôti de porc au pastis,*
> – *Alouettes sans tête,* "Headless" larks,
> – *Pot au feu provençal,* Provencal stew,
> – *Brigadèou,*
> – *Panisses.*

La daube

Beef stew

*S*OMETIMES it seems as though there are as many variations of this recipe as there are Provencal families. Here's ours :

Take 2 kg of beef (topside, ribs, or knuckle, all chopped into big pieces). For the marinade, take 1 litre of red wine, 1 glass of vinegar, 2 onions, 3 carrots, 1 bouquet garni, 1 bunch of rosemary and a few peppercorns.

To cook this dish, also take some olive oil, 1 handful of diced streaky bacon, 2 onions and 3 or 4 cloves of garlic as well as the zest of 1/3 of an orange and a lemon, and some salt.

If you can, cook your daube the day before. The more it is cooked, cooled down, and then reheated the better. It is the ideal dish in winter, cooked on an old range, as its aroma will spread throughout the house.

At least 5 or 6 hours beforehand, put the pieces of beef in the marinade made of wine, vinegar, onions, carrots, herbs and pepper.

In a thick-sided casserole dish, brown the diced streaky bacon with the roughly chopped onions. Strain the meat (but don't throw the marinade away) and brown it in the casserole dish.

Then, pour the marinade in it. Add the crushed garlic, the peels of the fruits and 1/2 litre of warm water. Cover and leave to cook for at least 4 hours.

Serve with a «*macaronade*» (see following page), or with steamed potatoes sprinkled with chopped parsley.

Macaronade

Macaroni au gratin

*A*PART *from the macaroni, take the gravy from a daube, or as an alternative any other gravy, some grated cheese (about a bowl-full), some breadcrumbs and a little butter.*

Cook the macaroni for 5 minutes in a lot of salted water, strain well and blend with the grated cheese. Pour into a buttered oven-proof dish and then pour over the gravy.

Sprinkle some breadcrumbs and a few knobs of butter on the top. Cook in the oven for 10 minutes.

Rôti de porc au pastis

*T*AKE *a joint of porc, 1 onion and 1 bowl of "coulis de tomate" (page 20), and, for the marinade, 1 glass of pastis (see "anisette" page 134), 1 glass of olive oil, 1 onion with a clove, 3 leaves of sage, some salt and pepper and a few aniseeds.*

Three hours before, place the joint in the marinade.

Strain and brown in a casserole dish with a little olive oil.

Add the marinade and the « coulis de tomate », cover, and leave to cook for one and a half hour.

This dish can also be prepared in a pressure cooker, in which case it will cook much more rapidly.

Alouettes sans tête

"Headless" larks

*I*F these "larks" are headless, it is because they are in fact only "olives".

For 6, take 800 gr/30 oz of beef, (chuck or topside). For the stuffing, take 250 g/10 oz of streaky bacon, 6 cloves of garlic, 1 bunch of parsley, some salt and pepper.

Take also some olive oil, 2 onions, 1 glass of white wine or red wine, 1 glass of "coulis de tomate" (see page 20) and 1 bouquet garni.

Cut 12 thin slices of the beef (2 per guest). If there is any left, include it in the stuffing : mince the bacon, the garlic and parsley, season and stir well.

Place the stuffing and each slice of beef, roll the meat and tie with string.

Brown each of these "alouettes" in a large casserole dish with some olive oil and the chopped onions. Water with the wine, then add the bouquet garni and the "coulis de tomate".

Leave to cook on a very slow heat for at least two hours. This dish is traditionally served with steamed potatoes, seasoned with salt and pepper and a dash of olive oil.

Pot au feu provençal

Provencal stew

*T*HIS dish will be equally as good cooked in a pressure cooker, which will reduce the cooking time. You can also skin the fat of this stew.

Take a pound of beef (chunk for instance), a pound of mutton, 2 or 3 marrowbones, 2 or 3 onions with a clove, 6 carrots, 2 sticks of celery, 2 cloves of garlic, 3 trimmed leeks, 1 handful of chickpeas (soaked for 12 hours), 1 bouquet garni, a few peppercorns, and juniper berries, some salt and six potatoes.

Place the meat in a large casserole dish, with cold salted water. Leave to cook until the water boils. Meanwhile, clean and peel the vegetables, except the potatoes, and chop them into large pieces. When the water boils, skin it and add the vegetables, the bouquet garni, the peppercorns and the juniper berries.

Leave to cook for 2 to 3 hours.

If you can (and have enough time for it), place the casserole and its lid with a stone on it outside, to that it cools down. You can then skin the fat off. Put the casserole back to cook for another 20 minutes with the peeled potatoes, split into two.

Serve with gerkhins and cooking salt, and toasted slices of bread to spread the marrow on. The vegetable left-overs, blended in the liquidizer with the stock, make an excellent soup.

Brigadeou

THIS used to be the poor man's porridge. once considered as a "vulgar dish cooked in the country" in the respectable cookery books, it is nonetheless very tasty.

The "brigadeou" is made with chickpea flour (you can find it in the market place, where the olives and the cod are sold, under the name of "farine de pois chiches") or with corn semolina or "polenta", in which case the dish is called "poulinte".

Take 250 g/10 oz of it, 1 litre of water, some salt, and a few large tablespoons of olive oil.

Put the salted water to the boil with the olive oil. Away from the heat, sprinkle the water with the flour, stirring all the time so as not to get any lumps. Still stirring, let it cook for about twenty minutes.

In the past, people used to stir with a small sprig of bay-tree, instead of a wooden spoon.

The "brigadeou" is served with a green salad and with a dash of olive oil or of spicy "coulis de tomate". It might also be sprinkled with grated cheese and served au gratin.

Panisses

THE **"panisses"** are made out of a thick "brigadèou", either prepared with less water, or cooked longer, and then left to cool down in small bowls.

Turn them out and fry them in olive oil for a few minutes until they achieve a golden colour and are crusty.

You can also pour the "brigadèou" into a large dish and, once it has cooled down, cut lozenges, which you can then fry accordingly.

CHAPTER 9

Cheese

*I*F Provence is not strictly speaking a cheese region, there is still a variety of goats'cheese that you can find here : "crottins", "pelardons", "picodons", "banons"… from one name to another and from one village to another, the flavour vary.

> – *Le chèvre versatile,*
> – *La brousse,*
> – *Crottins à l'huile d'olive,*
> – *Cachaï.*

Le chèvre versatile

*T*O taste this as its best, you'll have to recognise it at its best. For instance, the best **"banon"** are only found in Banon (the village), and each cheese maker has his own method. By dawdling in the market place, by knocking at the old sheepfolds'doors, under the sign **"Ici fromages de chèvres"** (*"Here goats'cheese"*), you will find your favourite fully ripened cheese. Each degree of maturity has its own use :

For an aperitif : spice some very fresh cheese with some ground pepper and mix it with a handful of herbs : parsley, chives…, etc.
Serve it on toast or with small sticks of celery or in scooped out cheery tomatoes.

For a dressing : mix some very fresh cheese with a yoghurt and a dash of olive oil.

In an omelette : crumble some fresh cheese in the eggs before cooking.

In a stuffing : with spinach and any left-overs used to stuff the ravioles (see page 62), vegetables or mushroom, choose it fresh.

In a salad : choose it very mature and cut it into slices to serve it with the dressing or prepare it on "roustide" : to do so, take one cheese for each guest and place it on a slice of farmhouse bread (**"pain de campagne"**) and grill, for a few minutes in the oven. Place each "roustide" on each guest's plate.

As a cheese, choose it fresh, creamy or very mature, serving it on vine leaves or fig leaves.

Decorate each cheese with savory, a black olive, a rolled anchovy or a few juniper berries.

La brousse

A COUSIN of the "brocciu" from Corsica and the "ricotta" from Italy, the **"brousse"** is a hardly curdled tomme, made of goats'milk or ewes'milk. You can find it in any market place or at the dairyman's, but it's nice to try and make it yourself...

Buy some curds and ask for 1 litre of goats'milk from any sheepfold. Take some spririt vinegar and a square of muslin (usually used to make butter), unless you already have a cheese mould.

Warm the milk in a clay vessel if you can, or in an enamelled saucepan. Turn off the heat before it boils. Add one teaspoonful of curds, and another of vinegar. Stir well and leave the milk to curdle in a warm place until the cheese comes away from the saucepan when titled.

Pour in a sieve with a piece of muslin in it and leave to strain. If you like your cheese dryer, tie the four corners of the muslin and hang for a few hours above the sink.

The brousse can be eaten with a little salt, or as a dessert, sweetened with honey and served with ground almonds.

Crottins
à l'huile d'olive

*T*HIS recipe enhances the flavour of goats' cheese. It also enables you to use the cheeses which are a little too dry.

Take a few jars, not too large, some savory, some thyme and a few bay-leaves, 2 or 3 chillies for each jar, some peppercorns, a lot of olive oil and enough cheese – dry ones if possible – to fill the jars.

The jars have to be clean and dry. Alternate the cheese with the seasoning, and cover with olive oil. Close the jars and wait one month before eating.

Cachaï

$\mathcal{T}$HE cachaï is a fermented cheese, usually made with cheese leftovers.

Take a clay pot and its lid, some Provencal marc brandy, some salt and pepper, a few aromatic herbs, according to your taste and some goats and ewe's cheese.

Pound the cheese with a glass of marc brandy, and season well, and store in the closed pot. Wait for at least one week before you taste it and serve it. This cheese quickly becomes very strong, which doesn't put off the cheese lovers who serve it on a slice of bread with a raw onion! You can fill the pot by little with the cheese crumbs pounded in the pot with what is already in the pot, and add a drop of marc brandy each time.

CHAPTER 10
Puddings and sweets

*T*HE plump fruits from Provence ripe in the garden, sweet and warm, are to be soon either "confits" (candied), a local speciality, or part of a pudding. The almonds are transformed into "calissons" or "nougats", and, traditionally, on Christmas Eve, there will be the "treize desserts" on the table.

Who can resist it?

- *À propos des treize desserts,* About the "treize desserts"
- *Nougat noir,* Dark nougat
- *Pompe à l'huile,*
- *Couronne des rois,*
- *À propos des fruits,* About fruits
- *Fruits confits,* Candied fruits
- *Millasson,*
- *Navettes,*
- *Cocos d'anis,*
- *Oreillettes ou merveilles,*
- *Chichis- fregis.*

About the "treize desserts"

*I*T IS the tradition, on Christmas Eve, before the *"messe de minuit"* (midnight mass), to eat "the big supper" called *"lou gros soupa"* in Provence. This is a meal without meat, but it is festive however : it is composed of cod, snails, aïoli, etc. and to finish it, the famous ***"treize desserts"***.

In the first place the *"pompe à huile"*, soaked into a liqueur wine. There always are four varieties of fresh fruits such as apple, peer, orange and pomegranate for instance, and five varieties of dried fruits, called *"mendiants"* uch as walnuts, hazelnuts, dried figs, dates, raisins, and pistachio nuts. Don't forget the nougats, white or black, some pieces of fruit jelly, or some candied fruits and jams.

Nougat noir
Dark nougat

*Y*OU *will only need 500 g/1lb of honey, 500 g/1 lb of almonds, and a dash of lemon juice for this recipe. Take some greaseproof paper, or more traditionally a sheet of host («hostie»), and a small rectangular tin.*

Mince half the almonds and cut the paper according to the tin dimensions, and oil it well. If you use an host sheet, moisten it before placing it into the tin.

Heat the honey in a saucepan, stirring all the time, until it is boiling and darkening. Throw all the almonds and the lemon juice in the saucepan. Heat while stirring for fifteen minutes, until the nougat becomes gold. It is then ready. Away from the heat, stir for a little longer before pouring the nougat into the tin. Leave it to harden in a cold room and cut it into pieces.

Pompe à l'huile

TAKE 500 g/1 lb of plain flour, 15 centilitres of olive oil, 25 g/1 oz of yeast, 100 g/4 oz of sugar, a tablespoon of orange blossom water, a pinch of salt, and if you like, a piece of orange peel or some aniseed.

The day before you cook the «pompe à huile», dilute the yeast into some warm water and add 125 g/5 oz of flour. Stir well and leave to stand for the whole night in a warm place.

Incorporate the olive oil, the sugar, the salt, the orange blossom water in the flour, as well as the water and yeast prepared the day before, and the piece of orange peel or the aniseed.

Knead the pastry on a floured piece of wood. The pastry must be soft, lump free and must not be sticky.

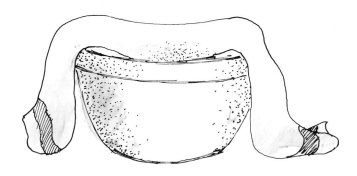

Cover the pastry with a clean cloth and allow it to stand for one hour. Knead the pastry once again. Flatten it with your hand and cut the surface four or six times with a knife. Carefully place the pompe à huile on the buttered and floured baking tray, cover it with a cloth and leave it to stand once again for one hour or two. Bake in a hot oven for twenty to twenty-five minutes.

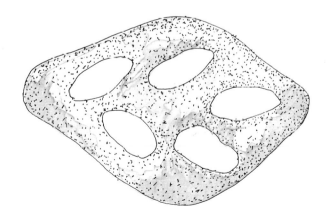

Couronne des rois

THIS is the pudding eaten in Provence to celebrate Twelfth Night. It is made with candied fruit, and a charm is hidden in it, for the King or Queen of the day to find.

Take 500 g/1 lb of plain flour, 20 g/1 oz of fresh yeast, 100 g/4 oz of sugar, three eggs, 100 g/4 oz of soft butter, a pinch of salt, some candied fruits and a charm (fève).

Dilute the yeast in a little warm water. Pour the flour in a salad bowl. To the eggs, add the sugar, the softened butter cut into pieces, and the salt. Stir well, while adding little by little the yeast and water.

Knead the pastry on a floured surface. It must be soft, lump free and must not feel sticky. Cover it with a clean cloth, and leave it to stand in a warm place for one hour.

Knead the pastry again. Make a ring of it and incorporate half of the chopped candied fruits in it, as well as the charm.

Place the "*couronne*" on the oiled and floured baking-tray and cover it with a cloth. Allow it to stand for one hour or two.

Bake it in a hot oven for about half an hour, decorate it with the other half of the candied fruits and icing or confectioner's sugar.

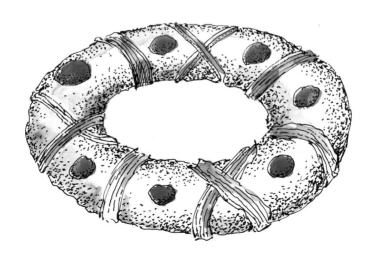

About fruits

FRUITS are always magnificent in Provence, but some are particularly well-known, such as melon, water melons, figs and grapes.

They're eaten at any time, chilled or still warm or they are prepared into stubtle and varied desserts. Here are some ideas :

Melons can be served in dice, with raspberries, sprinkled with a little « vin d'orange » (see page 138) or with a raspberry syrup, and served in the lemon peels.

Water melons can be served in the same way with any kind of grape.

Peers can be cooked in red wine with a little sugar and cinnamon for an hour.

Apricots can be baked into tarts. Divide them into halves placed on a shortcrust pastry, with a little sugar sprinkled over them and cooked in a hot oven for twenty minutes.

Apples and quinces can be cooked into a compote, and might be served with a vanilla ice-cream.

Fruits confits

Candied fruits

A SPECIALITY from Provence, they come from Apt, Carpentras, Aix-en-Provence. In Beaumes-de-Venise, you'll find apricots, in Cotignac, you'll discover figs and in Nice you can even buy a jam of candied-fruits!

To prepare the candied fruits at home is a long and delicate process. Here it is:

The fruits have to be perfect, hardly ripe, washed, cleaned, blanched, and drained.

They should then be cooked very briefly every other day, in a 15° syrup the first day, increasing by 2° or 3° each time so as to reach 32°.

The fruits should be drained a last time and stored carefully in paper-made boxes.

Millasson

*T*HIS rustic pudding, very easy and quick, was once made with millet flour, now replaced by cornflour.

Take 100 g/4 oz of cornflour, 200 g/7 oz of sugar, four eggs, a piece of orange peel and 3/4 of a litre of milk.

Heat the milk. In a salad bowl, pour the sugar, the flour and the minced orange peel. Fold in the eggs, and pour the boiling milk in the salad bowl. Stir well. The batter should be lump free. Pour it in a buttered flat tin and cook the millasson for about 20 minutes.

Serve it sprinkled with caster sugar.

Navettes

TAKE 500 g/1 lb of flour, 250 g/9 oz of caster sugar, a pinch of salt, 50 g/2oz of softened butter, 1/2 a tablespoon of orange blossom water, 3 eggs, 20 g/1oz of yeast.

Dilute the yeast in a little warm water. Pour the flour in a salad bowl, add the eggs to it and stir well. Then add the sugar, the butter cut into pieces, the orange blossom water, the salt and the yeast and water. Knead the pastry well and, as for the previous recipe, leave to stand for a while and knead again. Cut the pastry into 6 cm long cylinders, flatten them slightly and give them the form of pastry boats.

With a knife, make a hole in the middle of each one, place the "navettes" on the baking tray, and leave them to stand for another hour.

Glaze the "navettes" with an egg yolk or some milk and cook fifteen minutes in a hot oven, keeping an eye on them.

Cocos à l'anis

AKE 250 g/9 oz of caster sugar, 250 g/9 oz of flour, two eggs, a pinch of salt, and 12 g of aniseed.

Mix the sugar and the eggs in a salad bowl and add the flour, the salt and the aniseed.

Knead the pastry and roll it. Cut circle shapes with a glass and place each circle on a buttered baking tray. Cook in a slow oven for about 20 to 30 minutes, until the edges brown slightly.

Oreillettes ou merveilles

TAKE 500 g/ 1 lb of flour, four eggs, 1/2 glass of caster sugar, 1/2 glass of olive oil, 1/2 glass of orange blossom flower, 1/2 sachet of baking powder, a pinch of salt and some frying oil.

Pour the flour into the salad bowl, and then all the other ingredients, except the frying oil. Stir well, and leave to stand under a cloth for 2 hours.

Roll the paste in a very thin layer. With a pastry wheel, cut out the diamond shaped oreillettes, and either cut them in their middle, or twist them.

Fry them very briefly, drain them on kitchen paper, and sprinkle them with caster sugar or icing or confectioner'sugar.

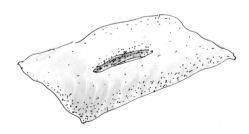

Chichis fregis

OR the paste, take 500 g/ 1 lb of flour, 1/2 sachet of baking powder, a pinch of salt, 2 tablespoons of orange blossom water, and 1 of caster sugar.

Mix the flour, the baking powder, the sugar, and the salt, with the orange blossom water, and enough warm water to obtain a soft paste.

Leave to stand for one hour under a cloth, and roll the paste into thin cylinders which you will throw in the boiling oil.

Drain them well on kitchen paper and roll the chichis in the sugar.

CHAPTER 11
Home - made drinks and jams

On the well ordered shelves, the corked bottles and the old jam jars are lined up, each one adding to the provision of small joys, all with hand-written labels. They will be served as an aperitif or a liqueur after dinner, or might make a perfect gift for a friend.

- *Anisette,* Pastis
- *Sirop d'orgeat,* Almond syrup
- *Rinquinquin,* Peach wine
- *Vin de sauge,* Sage wine
- *Eau de sauge,* Sage liqueur
- *Vin d'orange,* Orange wine
- *Ratafia de genièvre,* Juniper liqueur
- *Confiture d'oranges amères,* Bitter orange jam
- *Marmelade de melon,* Melon marmalade
- *Gelée de mures,* Blackberry jelly
- *Confiture de figues,* Fig jam.

Anisette

Pastis

*T*HIS pastis won't have a great name on its label, but the fact that it is home-made will certainly work in its favour.

In a bottle with a wide neck, drop 50 g/1,7 oz of aniseed, and a few star-shaped aniseed called "***anis étoilé***" or "***badiane***" in Provence, a liquorice stick, a twig of fennel, and a stick of cinnamon.

Cover with one litre of brandy, leave to macerate for one month, and filter.

At this stage, you can either leave the anisette as it is, or add to it a glass of syrup, made of 250 g/9 oz of sugar cooked in a glass of water. Bottle it.

Anisette can be served with water as an aperitif of course, but it also gives a nice flavour to many dishes, such as puddings, or more surprisingly meats such as "*rôti de porc*" (see page 101), for instance.

Sirop d'orgeat
Almond syrup

TAKE 500 g/1 lb of almonds, and 100 g/4 oz of bitter almonds, 500 g/1 lb of sugar, and 1/2 glass of orange blossom water.

Throw the almonds in boiling water, turn off the heat and leave to stand for two minutes. Drain the almonds, and remove their skins.

Blend the almonds in a mixer, adding a constant dash of water, so as to obtain 2 litres of almond milk.

Blend the milk again with the orange blossom water, and filter.

Heat the syrup in a bain-marie with the sugar until it is dissolved.

Bottle the syrup in well corked recipients and keep in a cold place.

Rinquinquin
ou vin de pêche
Peach wine

GATHER 40 leaves from a young and untreated peach tree. Macerate in a jar with 40 lumps of sugar, 2 litres of a nice red wine, and a glass of marc.

Leave to stand for 40 days in a dark place before fitting and bottling.

Vin de sauge
Sage wine

TONIC and fortifying, it is served as an aperitif and is reminiscent of some Greek wines.

In a bottle of good white wine, place a twig of sage and three tablespoons of liquid honey and cork.

Allow it to stand for three weeks before you taste it.

Eau de sauge
Sage liqueur

TO strengthen the previous version of the vin de sauge, the sage is this time macerated in brandy. Eight days later the filtered brandy is poured in the same quantity of sugar syrup.

Vin d'orange

Orange wine

*T*HIS is a classic, and a real treat, only to be prepared, however, with the untreated oranges of your garden.

In a big jar, macerate 1 bitter orange and 1 sweet one, both chopped into pieces, the quarter of a lemon, 1 litre of white wine, or rosé, 1 glass of marc, 200 g / 7 oz of caster sugar, and either some vanilla or some cinnamon. Leave 40 days to stand, filter, and bottle the wine.

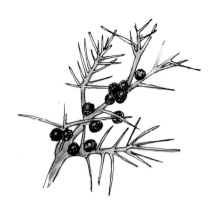

Ratafia de genièvre
Juniper liqueur

Take one handful of juniper berries, throw them with the finely chopped half of a lemon and cover the whole with one litre of brandy.
Make a syrup with 250 g/9 oz of sugar and half a litre of water.
Pour the syrup in the jar, stir well, and keep tightly corked for one month.
Filter and bottle.

Confiture
d'oranges amères
Bitter orange jam

*T*HIS jam takes a little while to prepare, but it will perfume your house while it is being cooked.

This recipe is for 1 kg / 2 lb of untreated oranges. Wash the fruits and slice them thinly. Remove the pips and tie them in a square of muslin. Place the fruits in a large jar with 2,5 litres of water and leave to soak for 12 hours. Pour the fruits and the water in a preserving pan, cook very slowly for 35 to 40 minutes, and pour back into the jar, and allow to stand for another 24 hours.

Weigh the cooked fruits and add the same amount of sugar. Cook again for 30 minutes, this time adding the square of muslin. Put the jam in jars.

Marmelade de melon
Melon marmalade

*T*HIS marmalade is often made when there are plenty of melons, and people just cannot throw them away.

Peel the melons and dice their pulp. Macerate in the refrigerator for a whole night, with the same weight of sugar.

To flavour the marmalade, add a finely sliced orange, a handful of red currants, or wild summer fruits.

Cook slowly until the marmalade thickens and takes a golden shade.

Gelée de mures

Blackberry jelly

*T*HIS recipe is very easy to prepare and it is so tasty that there are no reason to miss it; when there are plenty of blackberries along the sulken lanes. As well as the fruits and some sugar, you will need a square of muslin, or an old cloth.

Weigh the blackberries and cook them in a preserving pan with 1 glass of water for every pound of blackberries. As soon as the fruits burst, remove them from the heat.

Pour them through the cloth and sieve. Tie the cloth and hang it over the jar to collect the juice. You can squeeze the cloth if you wish to obtain a stronger flavour, but don't if you wish to obtain a limpid jelly.

Weigh the juice and add the same amount of juice and cook for 25 minutes.

Take the scum off and put in jars.

Confiture de figues
Fig jam

Take one pound of sugar for every kg/2 lb of figs and a lemon. Heat the sugar and the water for about 10 minutes until the syrup makes some small white bubbles and there is almost no liquid left.

Meanwhile, wash the figs and cut them into 4 pieces, and finely slice the lemon.

Throw the fruits in the syrup and cook for 30 to 40 minutes, before putting the jam into jars.

Published
in Spring 2000
as the young
rabbit was nibbling
savory in a Provencal
hill, without suspecting,
"peuchère", that he was to find
4 to 6 twigs of it in the casserole
dish, chopped into pieces with the liver
and the kidney, the olive oil,
a small tomato, 2 garlic cloves,
a dash of vinegar,
and some salt and
pepper. Poor
little rabbit!

Printing: Grafiche Zanini
2th edition